CONTENTS

CHAPTER ONE
A BIG SCARE 4
CHAPTER TWO
WHY WOULD
THEY ATTACK? 8
CHAPTER THREE
WHO WINS? 16
CHAPTER FOUR
NO REASON
TO BE AFRAID 22

Glossary 28
Trivia................................. 29
Activity 30
Find out more 32
Index................................. 32

CHAPTER 1

A BIG
Scare

People turned on their radios. It was a Sunday night in 1938. Televisions were not popular yet. People listened to radios for entertainment and the news.

BRIGHT
IDEA
BOOKS

WOULD WE
Survive
AN ALIEN
INVASION?

by Katie Chanez

Raintree is an imprint of Capstone Global Library Limited, a company incorporated in England and Wales having its registered office at 264 Banbury Road, Oxford, OX2 7DY – Registered company number: 6695582

www.raintree.co.uk
myorders@raintree.co.uk

Edited by Claire Vanden Branden
Designed by Becky Daum
Original illustrations © Capstone Global Library Limited 2020
Production by Melissa Martin
Originated by Capstone Global Library Ltd
Printed and bound in India

978 1 4747 8753 6 (hardback)
978 1 4747 8757 4 (paperback)

British Library Cataloguing in Publication Data
A full catalogue record for this book is available from the British Library.

Acknowledgements
We would like to thank the following for permission to reproduce photographs: iStockphoto: 3000ad, 9, 29, bertos, 21, 28, chainatp, 5, estt, 30–31, grandeduc, 14–15, gremlin, 24–25, Михаил Руденко, 18–19; NASA: PL-Caltech, 12–13; Shutterstock Images: 3000ad, cover, 26–27, Design Projects, 10–11, Fred Mantel, 6–7, Pavel Chagochki, 17, ra2studio, 23. Design elements: Shutterstock Images, Red Line Editorial.

Every effort has been made to contact copyright holders of material reproduced in this book. Any omissions will be rectified in subsequent printings if notice is given to the publisher.

All the internet addresses (URLs) given in this book were valid at the time of going to press. However, due to the dynamic nature of the internet, some addresses may have changed, or sites may have changed or ceased to exist since publication. While the author and publisher regret any inconvenience this may cause readers, no responsibility for any such changes can be accepted by either the author or the publisher.

The Sunday programme started the way it did every week. Then it suddenly took a turn. A news reporter said **aliens** were **invading** Earth. People began to run for safety.

The radio programme caused many people to panic. They believed aliens were attacking like this!

Many people want to have a plan in place in case aliens actually do invade Earth.

NO ATTACK

Roads became jammed with drivers trying to escape. People were crying. They thought they were going to die.

But there was no attack. It was just a **play**. The reporter was an actor called Orson Welles. The play was based on a book called *War of the Worlds*. Welles said that he never meant to scare anyone. Earth was safe. But people started to wonder. What would happen if Earth was really attacked? Would we survive?

WAR OF THE WORLDS

H. G. Wells wrote *War of the Worlds*. It was published in 1898.

CHAPTER 2

WHY WOULD They Attack?

People have ideas on why aliens might attack. Some think they might want Earth's water. Others think they want to study people. They might want to use humans as workers.

The surface of Earth is about 71 per cent water. Aliens might come to Earth because they have run out of water on their planet.

Aliens also might need a new place to live. They could have ruined their home. People have taken over other countries. They have started wars. Some think aliens could do the same.

Some people think aliens would want to take over the entire world.

Voyager 1 was launched in 1977. Its mission was to explore the edge of our **solar system**.

HOW WOULD THEY GET HERE?

Aliens would need spacecraft to reach Earth. They would need better spacecraft than humans have. Only two spacecraft from Earth have left our solar system. The first took 35 years. The second spacecraft took 41 years. It travelled far from Earth. This spacecraft has travelled more than 17.7 billion kilometres (11 billion miles).

Aliens would have to travel many **light years**. One light year is almost 9.6 trillion kilometres (6 trillion miles). Nothing on Earth is faster than the speed of light. Aliens would have to travel faster than light.

MILKY WAY

Earth is in the Milky Way galaxy. The Milky Way could be 200,000 light years wide.

Aliens would have to travel very far and very fast to reach Earth.

CHAPTER 3

WHO Wins?

Some people think we would lose the war against aliens. They could have better weapons. They could attack our computer systems. Computers control many weapons. Aliens could turn our weapons against us.

Some people think aliens could easily take over the world.

Spacesuits protect astronauts in outer space.

Other people think humans would win. Aliens come from far away. The air on Earth is different. People need special suits in space. Aliens might need them to survive on Earth.

DEADLY BACTERIA

The aliens died in *War of the Worlds*. Bacteria on Earth made them ill.

People could also win by fighting.
Countries use armies to fight in wars
on Earth. Armies could be used to fight
aliens. Or we could not fight at all.
We could talk to the aliens to find peace.

Many people think
that we could be
friends with aliens
and live together on
Earth in peace.

21

CHAPTER 4

NO REASON to Be Afraid

Scientists have not found alien life yet. But there may be plans in place if they do attack.

Most government plans are secret. But many people think there is a basic plan in place. First the government would tell everyone to stay at home. It would give orders over the TV or radio.

In an alien invasion emergency, the government might give information through newsreaders on television.

Then the government would try to talk to the aliens. It would see if they are friendly or not. We would find peace if the aliens were friendly. We would go to war if they meant to attack us.

If aliens came to Earth, the government would need to be very careful when it makes contact. It wouldn't want to anger the aliens.

Alien invasions are still just ideas in science fiction films for now.

But most scientists don't think we should be afraid. Aliens might be scared of people. We might reach them first. We could hurt them by accident.

Aliens might not even want to come to Earth. Do you think they will come one day? What do you think would happen if they did?

GLOSSARY

alien
creature not from Earth

bacteria
tiny germs that can make
people or animals sick

galaxy
large groups of stars and
solar systems in the universe

light year
how far light can travel in one
year; a measurement used
in space

play
performance of a story

solar system
sun and the planets and other
bodies that revolve around it

TRIVIA

1. Orson Welles became a famous film director after his radio performance of *War of the Worlds* caused mass panic.

2. Many groups have tried to contact aliens. They have not received any messages so far.

3. The National Aeronautics and Space Administration (NASA) has a department called the Office of Planetary Protection. One of its jobs is to make sure bacteria is not accidentally spread between planets.

ACTIVITY

COME UP WITH YOUR OWN ALIEN INVASION!

Write a story or draw a comic about an alien invasion. Describe your aliens. Why are they attacking Earth? How are they attacking? Now switch to the humans. What are they doing to defend themselves?
Who wins? Why?

FIND OUT MORE

Books

Aliens and UFOs (Solving Mysteries with Science), Lori Hile (Raintree, 2013)

Can You Survive an Alien Invasion? (You Choose: Doomsday), Blake Hoena (Raintree, 2015)

Have Aliens Visited Earth? (Top Secret!), Nick Hunter (Raintree, 2017)

Paranormal Handbook to UFOs, Crop Circles and Alien Encounters, Sean McCollum (Raintree, 2016)

Websites

Do aliens really exist?
www.bbc.co.uk/newsround/19840847

Learn more about space from the European Space Agency.
www.esa.int/kids/en/home

INDEX

aliens 5, 8, 10, 13–14, 16, 19–20, 22, 24, 27

attacks 7, 8, 22, 27

Earth 5, 7, 8, 13, 14, 19–20, 27

governments 23–24

light years 14

Milky Way 14

radios 4, 23

spaceships 13

war 10, 16, 20, 24

War of the Worlds 7, 19

Welles, Orson 7